Introduction

Welcome to **Bill's New Frock**, a two-part drama specially commissioned by **Channel 4 Schools**. It has been adapted for television by Andrew Davies from the book of the same name by award-winning author, Anne Fine.

In the story, Bill Simpson wakes up one morning to find that he has turned into a girl. His mother insists that he wears a pretty pink frock to school. As Bill's dreadful day unfolds, one horror following another, his bizarre and hilarious experiences reveal just how utterly ridiculous gender constraints are.

The curriculum throughout the UK places great emphasis on pupils developing as enthusiastic, independent and reflective readers. **Book Box** provides teachers with strong support in developing key skills in English, related to reading and to speaking and listening.

The range of activities suggested will support the literacy curriculum in general and the Literacy Hour in particular. Reading and writing activities have been specifically designed to provide follow-up for the whole-class viewing of the programme.

We hope you will continue to enjoy this exciting series, which is intended to help and encourage children to keep closer company with books. Please send any comments, suggestions or examples of children's work to the address below. They are always most welcome.

Rick Hayes
Education Officer
Channel 4 Schools
PO Box 100
WARWICK
CV34 6TZ

The curriculum requirements for 7–11 year olds throughout the UK lay great stress on pupils being given opportunities to enjoy literature, and to study it in some detail. Much of pupils' reading at this age will quite rightly involve rapid individual encounters with books which pupils will read once and then move on. However, teachers will want to choose some books for closer study, to be shared by the whole class.

It is here that **Book Box**, with its focus on literature, can play an important role.

There are, of course, important differences between the way a story is told in print and on the screen. The existence of a piece of literature in two versions gives opportunities for closer study of the way characters are presented, issues discussed and narrative structured in both.

CONTENTS

♪ **Subtitles**
This **Channel 4 Schools** series is subtitled on Teletext for the deaf and hearing-impaired.

Bill's New Frock Episode 1

Programme outline

One morning Bill Simpson wakes up to find his worst nightmare has come true. He has turned into a girl. No one else in the family seems to react to this and his mother sends him to school wearing a pink dress. Everyone treats him differently on his way to school: Mean Malcolm, the local bully, and his henchman Sean Scab wolf whistle at him; and when he gets to school Mr Platworthy, the Headteacher, speaks much more gently to Bill than to the boys. The nightmare has just begun. Baffled by the way things are different for girls, Bill falls headlong into trouble. When, to everyone's amazement, he takes up a dare and kicks a ball through the Head's window, Bill thinks the end is in sight. What will Mr Platworthy do when he discovers that the culprit is the girl in the pink frock?

Before viewing

▶ Explain that the children will be watching a two-part dramatisation of the children's story, **Bill's New Frock,** by the popular author, Anne Fine. Discover whether or not the children are already familiar with her work. They may also have seen the adaptations of *Goggle Eyes* and *Madame Doubtfire/Mrs Doubtfire.*

▶ Explain that the original text has been adapted by Andrew Davies for television. Discuss the role of scriptwriters. Can the children anticipate the difficulties and opportunities they may experience? How closely would they expect the script to mirror the original? Remind the children of Andrew Davies' other recent television adaptations (such as *Pride and Prejudice*).

▶ You may wish to read the book to the children before viewing, especially if you wish to emphasise the contrast between the script and original.

▶ You may wish to explore the children's attitudes to gender issues before viewing the drama. What do they consider to be the advantages and disadvantages of being a boy or girl?

Whilst viewing

▶ Ask the children to consider special effects and techniques not available to an author. Do they enhance or detract from the story? The impact will be stronger if the children are already familiar with the story.

▶ Ask the children to observe any changes between the original and the adaptation.

▶ Ask the children to try hard to imagine themselves in Bill's situation and to consider the events from his point of view.

After viewing
Points for discussion 💬

It may be interesting to vary group formation. All girl, all boy and mixed groups may well report back differently, which will stimulate further discussion.

▶ What do the children consider to be the main themes of Anne Fine's story?

▶ Ask the children to discuss the main events of the drama and how they affect Bill now he is a 'girl'. How different would these events have been had he been a 'boy' or if a girl had suddenly become a 'boy'?

▶ Can the children pinpoint different vocabulary and attitudes in the way Bill is addressed and treated as a 'girl'? How are boys treated differently in the drama? Is the impact different in the television adaptation? It might be useful to read Chapter 1 to the class as a comparison.

▶ Astrid begins to emerge as a 'tomboy'. Andrew Davies refers to her, in the script, as a feminist. How do the children respond to this role? (cf. other 'tomboys' in children's stories, for example, Georgina (George) in Enid Blyton, Georgiana in *Georgiana and the Dragon* and other heroines in Judy Corbalis' writing, etc.) How do children view gentle, more passive boys? What is their role?

▶ What differences have the children observed between the original story and its adaptation?

Daniel Lee, who plays Bill

Drama/role-play

▶ Children could select certain main events from this episode and re-enact them with Bill playing a traditional male role. As an alternative, one of the female characters could become a 'boy'. Girls would then actively experience the reverse scenario which should enhance their enjoyment of the drama.

▶ Retell the story of *Rapunzel*. Groups may enjoy recrafting the story to give Rapunzel an active role in the story. If this is successful, the activity could be extended by adapting other well-known traditional stories, giving passive heroines a more dominant role. Children may enjoy hearing modern 'fairy stories' which have successfully changed the traditional female role, such as *The Wrestling Princess* and other stories by Judy Corbalis. There are interesting exceptions, like *Alice in Wonderland*.

Creative writing

▶ More able children may enjoy the challenge of readapting traditional stories, as above, but in writing. This could be done either individually or in pairs. It could be presented as a story or script to be acted out.

▶ Children could create further events in which Bill experiences life as a 'girl'. Read one or two extracts from the book to demonstrate the tight structure of Anne Fine's writing. Opening sentences could be offered to help the children come straight to the point.

▶ Activity sheet 1 is an extract from the Andrew Davies screenplay. Children could be asked to rewrite this episode in story form. Their results could then be compared with the Anne Fine original.

▶ Activity sheet 2 is offered to enable less able children to produce a piece of written work. Similar supplementary sheets could be devised.

Language

▶ Activity sheet 3 introduces a range of adjectives with traditional gender connotations. Children should write each word in the appropriate article of clothing representative of gender. If they feel a word has no bias it should be written in both articles. This exercise could be used to introduce or reinforce study of adjectives. Discussion groups could compare results. A pictorial display of the class decision could serve as a word bank.

▶ Activity sheet 4 is based on Chapter 1 of the book. The extracts are in random order and show the variety of alternatives to the word 'said' used by the author. Thirteen of the examples underlined need to be changed. Children can be reminded of or introduced to the skill of scanning. Additionally, the exercise can be used to introduce or reinforce the role of verbs. How can these nuances in language be reflected on television?

Media

▶ Activity sheet 5 contrasts the opening sequences of the book and the script. Children could be asked to discuss the differences and the effectiveness of each approach. More able children might like to adapt the opening of another story into a screenplay for television.

Art

▶ Groups could discuss ways of depicting the main events of the story in a classroom frieze. Smaller groups could then be allocated responsibility for a particular section and finished work displayed on this backdrop. This work could be developed further after viewing Episode 2.

CDT/maths/PSE/geography

▶ Activity sheet 6 offers space to design a playground which could be enjoyed equally by boys and girls. Younger children could be introduced to the layout of plans. More able/older children may be encouraged to use simple scale. 3-D models of the original design could be constructed. There is an opportunity, if appropriate, for this activity to be based on actual school needs and developed into a more in-depth cross-curricular project. Surveys of class or whole school opinion could be carried out. Space is also allocated for children to draw up an appropriate list of playground rules. This work could be carried out individually, in pairs, or in larger groups.

EXT. PLAYGROUND. DAY

Over with the girls, as SUSIE runs up:

ASTRID	**What are they on about?**
SUSIE	**Rohan's dared Martin to kick the ball through Mr Platworthy's window, but he won't do it.**
ASTRID	**Dead easy kick, that is.**
SUSIE	**Yes, but what if you got caught?**
BILL	**I'll do it.**
ASTRID	*Really?*
BILL	**Yeah! Just you watch.**

He marches across the playground to where the boys are. BOYS stare in astonishment as he marches up to MARTIN.

BILL	**Give us the ball, Mart.**

He takes it as he says it. MARTIN too astonished to resist.

MARTIN	**Hey! Give it *back*.**

He grabs for it, but BILL holds on, clutching it to him, and wrenches free.

BILL	**I'm taking the dare. What's the bet?**
ROHAN	**Nothing.**
BILL	*What's the bet?*

ROHAN holds up the bag of Monstergobbles.

BILL	**Right. Stand back.**

He places the ball. An awed crowd of both sexes stands at a respectful distance. BILL goes back a few paces. The open window gapes invitingly. BILL takes a run at it, and kicks.

Slow motion special effects would be nice with sound to enhance the effect as the ball hums through the air, curving slightly, and whooshes through the window. We can hear a series of bangs as it bounces about inside the room.

Then a CHEER goes up which is cut short abruptly as MR PLATWORTHY appears at the window.

MR PLATWORTHY	(Thunders) **Stand still, boys and girls! Not a word. Not a whisper. If anyone so much as moves a muscle…**
	Now, WHO KICKED THAT BALL?

Bill Simpson

Bill is	a dog a teacher a boy
One day he wakes up as	a girl a boy a frog
His mother makes him put on	a hat a frock a vest
The frock is	big pink long
He goes to	town school bed
At school he kicks a ball through	a door a gate a window
He does it for	a joke a dare a friend

Now copy out the sentences to make a story:

_____

_____

_____

_____

_____

_____

On another sheet of paper draw a picture of Bill in his dress to put with your story.

Girl or Boy?

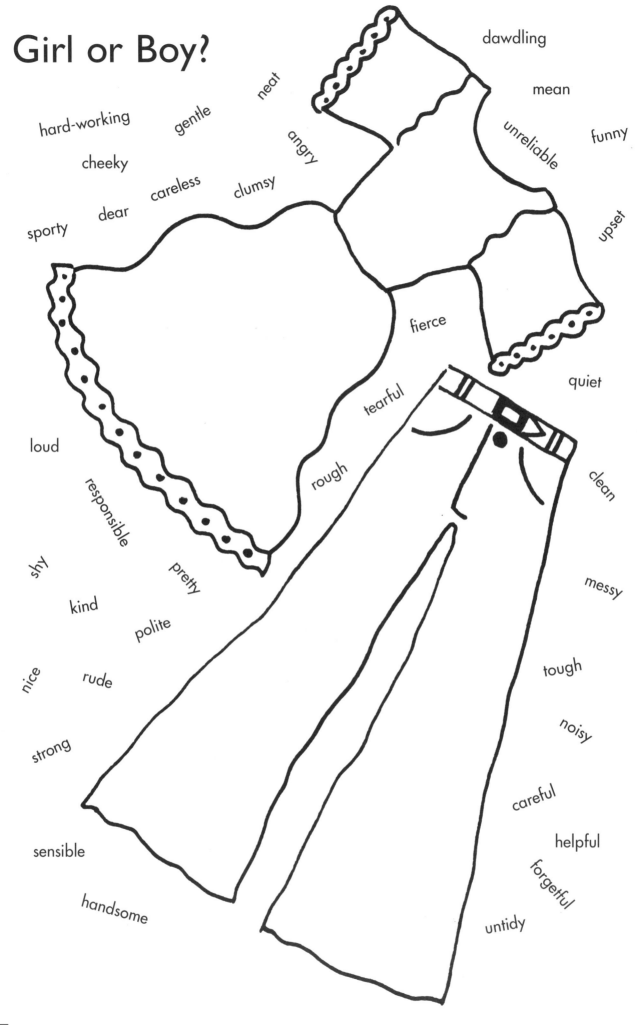

neat

dawdling

hard-working   gentle

mean

cheeky   angry

unreliable   funny

careless   clumsy

dear

sporty   upset

fierce

loud   tearful

quiet

rough   clean

responsible

shy   messy

kind   pretty

polite

nice   rude

tough

noisy

strong   careful

helpful

sensible   forgetful

handsome   untidy

Book Box **Bill's New Frock** Episode 1

Different voices

1 'No, really,' said Bill. 'I'm fine, honestly. I cross here every day by myself.'

2 'Stop fidgeting with your frock, dear,' she said to him.

3 'Oooooh!' Bill said…

4 'It isn't fair!' he said bitterly.

5 'Look at this,' she said…

6 'Get your skates on, Stephen Irwin!' he said.

7 'I *never* wear dresses,' Bill said…

8 'Now I need four strong volunteers to carry a table across to the nursery,' said the headmaster.

9 'Perhaps the table's quite heavy,' said Mrs Collins.

10 'Where are we?' she said.

11 'I don't see why Rapunzel just has to sit and wait for the Prince to come along and rescue her,' said Bill.

12 'Late, Andrew!' the headmaster said … fiercely.

13 'On with your work down there on table five,' said Mrs Collins promptly.

14 'Why don't you wear this pretty pink dress?' she said.

Book Box **Bill's New Frock** Episode 1

Different beginnings

Bill's New Frock

screenplay by Andrew Davies

TITLE: DREAM SEQUENCE

EXT. STREET. DAY

A long straight road of terraced houses. We are looking straight down it: exaggerated perspective, unearthly light.

BILL is running down the middle of the street in his pyjamas and slippers.

He is being pursued by a pink dress, flying steadily along about five feet off the ground.

BILL looks behind and sees the dress is gaining on him.

He is terrified.

The pink dress fill the screen – it is fighting its way over BILL's arms and body. For a split second we see BILL in the dress with his mouth open.

INT. BILL'S BEDROOM. NIGHT.

BILL jerks bolt upright in bed, in his pyjamas yelling:

BILL: Waagh!

TITLES: BILL'S NEW FROCK

Bill's New Frock

by Anne Fine

A Really Awful Start

When Bill Simpson woke up on Monday morning, he found he was a girl. He was still standing staring at himself in the mirror, quite baffled, when his mother swept in.

'Why don't you wear this pretty pink dress?' she said.

Bill's new playground

PLAYGROUND RULES

Bill's New Frock Episode 2

Programme outline

Things turn from bad to worse for Bill. During a wet lunchtime he has a fight in the classroom with his best friend Rohan Price over sharing comics (the *Bunty* and *Beano*). Bill has to get changed with the girls for a PE lesson. But when he and Astrid beat the boys during PE, Bill begins to think that being a girl might not be so bad after all. They even talk about starting a girls' football team. Is he starting to feel like a girl? Bill goes home confused and frustrated. When Mean Malcolm whistles at him it's the last straw. He arrives home in a ruined frock and is allowed to change out of it. All is resolved when he wakes next day.

Before viewing

▶ Children should be encouraged to recap on the events of Episode 1. What do they anticipate will be the outcome of the drama?

▶ If the children have already heard the story, they could usefully consider Andrew Davies' role again. Which events would they expect him to highlight in the second episode? Would any events not adapt so well to television and be omitted?

▶ You may wish to read the second half of the story at this stage to allow for comparison.

Whilst viewing

▶ Ask the children to consider technical effects. Encourage them to be aware of the use of music, lighting, voice overs, special effects. Are the scenes shot on location or in a studio?

▶ How does Bill's character develop in the second half of the story? How important are the secondary characters in the drama? Are the characters as they imagined from reading the book first?

▶ Ask the children to continue to identify any changes between the original and the adaptation.

After viewing

Points for discussion 💬

As before, it may be interesting to vary the make-up of the groups: all-boy, all-girl and mixed groups may bring out interesting variations in thought.

▶ Groups could be asked to compile lists of technical effects used in the drama. They could then assess the effectiveness of each of these. Were they able to identify scenes shot on location and those filmed in a studio?

▶ Ask the groups to consider characters. How many minor characters are there? Are they important to the drama? Were any performances particularly strong or particularly weak? Why do the children think that Andrew Davies invented a sister for Bill? Was it necessary? Why do they think he changed Bill's name to 'Billie' – did they like this idea?

▶ Why do the children think Anne Fine makes a point of mentioning the cat's behaviour at the beginning and end of the story?

▶ What changes to the story has Andrew Davies made in his adaptation? Do the children like these differences? Would they make any changes to his script? Would they have left out the children's race?

▶ Bill says to Mean Malcolm, 'I am not a dog … I am a person.' What do the children think is important about this statement? What does it tell them about changes in Bill's attitude?

▶ Do the children have any observations to make about the behaviour of Bill's parents? This theme of apparent parental indifference can also be observed in *Not Now, Bernard* by David McKee and the *Treehorn* stories by Florence Parry Heide.

▶ Children could be asked to pinpoint which particular events in the story play a part in altering Bill's own awareness of gender issues. What makes him become more sympathetic towards the girls in his class? In what ways are the boys equally discriminated against? Can the children remember any experiences in their own lives which reflect similar discrimination?

▶ The role of Bill in this drama is crucial. Do the children feel this actor was right for the part? Was he as they imagined Bill would be? If not, did this spoil their enjoyment of the drama?

Language

Speaking and Listening

▶ In circle time children could be invited to play a memory game: 'Bill felt in his pocket and found a penknife…' The next child repeats this, adding an item of his/her own choice, and so on, repeating everything which is already on the list.

▶ Everyone could be given the name of an item found in a child's pocket. Each would be given a short time to describe it, without revealing the name, while the other children try to guess its identity.

▶ The teacher describes ten items found in Bill's pocket. The children should try to guess the identity of the ten items in a list, working alone or in groups.

▶ Taking on the role of the teacher, and using activity sheet 7, the children should find as many ways as possible of reforming the class into two sets [cf Chapter 6].

▶ Two word searches are offered on activity sheet 8. The second is for more able/older children. Children can score out the answers or give the location of each word as co-ordinates. Answers are given on the inside back cover.

Alphabetical order

▶ Activity sheet 9 represents the medical forms dropped by Bill. Children should be asked to cut out the forms and make a pile in alphabetical order to hand back to the secretary. More simple/complex versions of this work could be devised as differentiated material.

Creative writing

▶ Empty the contents of a jacket pocket in front of the children. Ask them individually, in pairs or in groups to create a story including the items as part of the plot. This could be presented in a very simple or complex way, according to ability.

▶ Remind the children of the format of a script, using the given example (activity sheet 1). Now ask the children to adapt the story of the race, Chapter 6, as a screenplay.

▶ Ask the children to assess the structure and merits of two comics – one designed for boys and one traditionally thought of as a girls' publication, using activity sheet 10 as a guide. They could then design and present a story in comic strip form – possibly specifying that boys should choose a female 'hero', while girls give the leading role to a boy.

Drama

▶ A child joins the class: this person is very shy, has a disability or is in some way different. Children should produce two alternative playlets, one in which the child is made to feel comfortable, the second in which the reverse is true.

Media

▶ Encourage children to compare advertisements with particular regard to gender in the perceived messages. Children could then design their own advertisements with or without gender bias.

Maths

▶ The word searches on activity sheet 8 offer a practical task in the use of co-ordinates. Similarly, a survey on a gender issue, such as 'Do boys and girls have the same fears?' could offer opportunities for developing use of pie charts, bar charts, graphs, etc.

CDT/art

▶ Design an outfit suitable for boys and girls and including pockets. Paper models could be constructed and worn in a fashion parade to be assessed for practicality, attractiveness, etc. Children should be involved in deciding on preconditions: it must be suitable for school, only specified materials may be used, etc. Where appropriate, this work would link well with a study of male/female costume worn in other societies and cultural groups or at other times in history.

History/geography/PSE

▶ Activity sheet 11 addresses gender issues. Children could underline, circle or highlight in red statements with which they agree, in blue those with which they disagree and leave blank those on which they have no opinion. Groups can then form to discuss any uncertainties.

▶ Activity sheet 12 serves as a starting point to children for research into gender issues. Encourage children to choose as subjects men and women of different age groups and include themselves. Any comments can be recorded and relayed to the class.

▶ An obvious link with the above would be the study of the perceived role of men and women in other cultures and in other periods of history. Such a study could form part of the class cross-curricular topic where appropriate.

Who races against whom?

	FINISH

>	>	>	>	>	>
>	Those who like cats best > those who prefer dogs	>	>	>	>
>	>	>	>	>	Boys v Girls
1	**2**	**3**	**4**	**5**	**6**

START

Book Box **Bill's New Frock** Episode 2

Word search 1

	A	B	C	D	E	F	G	H	I
10	T	U	C	O	M	I	C	F	D
9	P	V	C	S	C	H	O	O	L
8	S	A	M	K	R	T	I	P	R
7	O	E	I	W	F	R	O	C	K
6	P	S	V	N	D	B	A	L	L
5	P	I	R	N	T	M	D	C	A
4	B	T	N	R	F	I	G	H	T
3	I	L	K	K	O	Y	B	B	U
2	L	T	R	G	I	R	L	O	F
1	L	R	O	E	L	N	O	Y	Y

Girl

Boy

Bill

Frock

School

Comic

Paint

Fight

Pink

Ball

Word search 2

Caretaker
Inks
Nurse
Medical forms
Mrs Collins
Bill
Dare
Mr Platworthy
Playground
Rohan
Paint
Comics
Astrid
Fight
Balls
Girls
Boys
Frock
Pink
Mean Malcolm

	1	2	3	4	5	6	7	8	9	10	11	12	13	14
15	R	P	L	A	Y	G	R	O	U	N	D	P	R	N
14	K	M	E	A	N	M	A	L	C	O	L	M	D	C
13	N	S	M	S	S	R	G	I	R	L	S	I	D	F
12	I	T	R	T	P	A	I	N	T	O	R	C	S	M
11	P	P	P	C	N	U	R	S	E	T	B	Y	I	R
10	O	L	L	K	A	T	R	U	S	U	O	N	G	S
9	A	A	A	O	J	R	C	A	R	B	B	L	H	C
8	P	Y	T	F	A	D	E	M	F	R	O	C	K	O
7	C	F	W	I	E	Y	N	T	C	D	N	O	A	L
6	D	R	O	G	O	P	P	C	A	A	R	N	C	L
5	H	O	R	H	D	A	R	E	H	K	L	T	O	I
4	S	U	T	T	L	T	O	O	H	W	E	R	M	N
3	K	N	H	I	M	X	R	B	N	Y	O	R	I	S
2	N	D	Y	B	I	L	L	B	A	L	L	S	C	F
1	I	M	E	D	I	C	A	L	F	O	R	M	S	W

4 SCHOOLS

Book Box **Bill's New Frock** Episode 2

Can you help Bill?

SMITH, Ann

JONES, David

ROLANDS, Peter

WILLIAMS, Steven

ANDREWS, Brian

SIDDHU, Anwar

CAMERON, Jenny

TRENT, Alison

PRINCE, Sylvia

MARCO, Antonio

HARRISON, Ian

Book Box **Bill's New Frock** Episode 2

Compare your comics

Comic 1

TITLE:

The main characters
How many boys? ____
How many girls? ____
Other ____

Story No. 1 is called

The 'HERO' is
Boy ____
Girl ____
Other ____

The main characters
How many boys? ____
How many girls? ____
Other ____

It is about

Story No. 2 is called

It is about

Story No. 3 is called

It is about

The 'HERO' is
Boy ____
Girl ____
Other ____

The main characters
How many boys? ____
How many girls? ____
Other ____

Story No. 4 is called

The 'HERO' is
Boy ____
Girl ____
Other ____

Evaluation
Fair to girls ____/10
Fair to boys ____/10
Enjoyment ____/10

Comic 2

TITLE:

The main characters
How many boys? ____
How many girls? ____
Other ____

Story No. 1 is called

The 'HERO' is
Boy ____
Girl ____
Other ____

The main characters
How many boys? ____
How many girls? ____
Other ____

It is about

Story No. 2 is called

It is about

Story No. 3 is called

It is about

The 'HERO' is
Boy ____
Girl ____
Other ____

The main characters
How many boys? ____
How many girls? ____
Other ____

Story No. 4 is called

The 'HERO' is
Boy ____
Girl ____
Other ____

Evaluation
Fair to girls ____/10
Fair to boys ____/10
Enjoyment ____/10

What do you think?

Men don't show their feelings.

Football is a man's game.

There is no point girls working hard at school – their place is in the home.

Women are bad drivers.

Girls hate getting dirty.

Girls should leave work like engineering to men.

Women are gentler than men.

Girls can be excellent at football.

There are men and women who are excellent drivers.

Loving is silly.

There are many men who look after homes and children.

Tough men sort things out with their fists.

Some men are bad drivers.

Men make better leaders.

Men shouldn't hit other men.

Many women do not like cleaning and cooking.

Men shouldn't hit women.

No real man would ever become a ballet dancer.

To be a ballet dancer a man needs to be fit and strong.

Girls are better at housework.

It's good for a man to cry if he is unhappy.

Girls are neater than boys.

Boys can be neat.

Some boys are very gentle and caring.

Everybody needs a cuddle sometimes.

The best chefs are men.

Some men make excellent nurses.

People should be paid the same if they do the same work whether they are women or men.

All boys like to be dirty.

Book Box **Bill's New Frock** Episode 2

SCHOOLS

Men, women or both?

Name of Activity	Name 1	Name 2	Name 3	Name 4	You	Any comments
Do the washing						
Change baby's nappy						
Repair the car						
Wear trousers						
Go out to work						
Clean the toilet						
Go to a football match						
Do the food shopping						
Wallpaper a room						
Wash up						
Go to watch a ballet						
Mop the floor						
Mend a bicycle						
Babysit						
Read to children						
Buy flowers						
Learn to dance						
Play on a rugby team						
Play with dolls						
Use a computer						
Ride a motorbike						
Write Christmas cards						
Dig the garden						

KEY   men – m   women – w   both – b

About the author: Anne Fine

I was sent to school two years early because my mother had triplets so can't remember a time when I couldn't read. I do remember every library I have ever used, though. I was one of those children librarians see coming. 'Look! Here she is again! Wasn't she here this morning?'

I wrote my first book when my eldest daughter was a baby. Trapped in our freezing flat by a snowstorm I started to write *The Summer House Loon* to cheer and warm myself up. It was finished in weeks. It was by far the fastest book I've ever written – and the sunniest.

Mostly, I write comedy. I think this is because my favourite books when I was a child were comedies: Richmal Crompton's *William* books, Anthony Buckeridge's *Jennings* books. I was also a great Enid Blyton fan. English was my favourite subject all through school, and I was good at it. I'm not sure I'd enjoy it if I were young now, though, with so much drafting and redrafting. We were allowed just to write, and we never had to go back to anything a second time except to correct spellings.

I've now written about twenty-five books for all ages, even adult. I still work as I always have: in absolute silence, hiding my work with my arms from anyone who comes in the room. I write with a 2B pencil and rub out constantly. (Don't mind redrafting now!) I have a special sharpener that catches the droppings for use on trains, but I can't help the manky bits of rubber getting all over the trays and tables, and I pity the person who gets my seat after.

I live by the side of a river in a tiny town in County Durham. I have two daughters, two unspeakable cats and a golden retriever.

The Anne Fine profile

How long does it take you to write a book?

For readers of ten and up, around a year. My adult novels have taken closer to two years.

Why don't you have a word processor?

I think most writers have a natural speed, and the work can suffer if they go faster. The speed I go suits me. As Americans say, 'If the recipe works, why fix it?'

What's your worst fault?

The bath – definitely. I spend hours and hours in the bath, reading.

Have you won any prizes?

Goggle Eyes won the Carnegie Medal and the Guardian Children's Fiction Award. *Bill's New Frock* won the Smarties Prize. *The Angel of Nitshill Road* was shortlisted for the 1993 Carnegie Medal, and *Flour Babies* won both the Carnegie and the Whitbread.

What would you rescue from a burning house?

My family, obviously, then my dog. (I hope I wouldn't be tempted to leave the cats…) Then the notes for the book I'm working on. (The carbons for what I've written already are safe in the car boot.)

What do you hate most in the entire world?

People sniffing (especially on trains).

What advice would you give to a would-be writer?

Read, read, read. The practice for writing is not writing, but reading. If you don't have a library card (and not in the teapot on the mantelpiece) you cannot be serious. Then, as Philip Larkin said, write the book you yourself would most like to read.

About the scriptwriter: Andrew Davies

My books and TV series for children include *Conrad's War, Alfonso Bonzo*, and six books about Marmalade Atkins. I also write television scripts for adults, such as *Pride and Prejudice, Moll Flanders* and the situation comedy, *Game On*.

I live in Kenilworth, Warwickshire, in an old house with a big garden and a snooker table in the cellar. My wife, Diana, used to be a teacher, and is now an art student. We have two children, Bill and Anna, but they are grown up now and don't live at home any more. Bill used to play in a band called SLAB! but now he teaches acoustics at Salford University. Anna is a script editor at Yorkshire TV, working on *Heartbeat*. We have three pets: two young black cats called Pansy and Molly, and a greyhound-cross dog (a lurcher) called Megan. They were all strays or abandoned when young.

I started off working as a teacher in schools in London, then worked at Warwick University training student teachers, and since 1987 I've been writing full-time. On a normal day I get up early, about seven, have breakfast, three days a week go to gym and work out (I am always a bit too fat because I'm too fond of food and drink), and try to get on the old word processor by nine or ten. The pets keep me company. I used to have a lot of hobbies like playing the guitar badly, trying to learn the saxophone, tap dancing, art, but I don't seem to do any of them now. I do love to play tennis right through the year, except when it's snowing.

I get a lot of inspiration from people and animals I know: for example, *Conrad's War* was inspired by my son, Bill, who was obsessed with war when he was in junior school. My advice to young writers is to think of the things in your own life that are funny or unusual or not quite like anything you've read in a book or seen on TV – with just a little bit of tweaking you can get a really original story out of them. And, if all else fails, have a hungry lion come through the classroom door.